BLACK
ACHIEVEMENTS
IN ACTIVISM

**CELEBRATING LEONIDAS H. BERRY,
MARLEY DIAS, AND MORE**

DR. ARTIKA R. TYNER
CICELY LEWIS, EXECUTIVE EDITOR

Lerner Publications ◆ Minneapolis

LETTER FROM CICELY LEWIS

Dear Reader,

As a girl, I wanted to be like Oprah Winfrey. She is a Black woman from Mississippi like me who became an award-winning actor, author, and businessperson. Oftentimes, history books leave out the accomplishments and contributions of people of color. When you

CICELY LEWIS

see someone who looks like you and has a similar background excelling at something, it helps you to see yourself be great.

I created Read Woke to amplify the voices of people who are often underrepresented. These books bring to light the beauty, talent, and integrity of Black people in music, activism, sports, the arts, and other areas. As you read, think about why it's important to celebrate Black excellence and the achievements of all people regardless of race, gender, or status. How did the people mentioned succeed despite barriers placed on them? How can we use these stories to inspire others?

Black excellence is everywhere in your daily life. I hope these people inspire you to never give up and continue to let your light shine.

With gratitude,

Cicely Lewis

TABLE OF CONTENTS

Protesters at the
Lincoln Memorial
on August 28, 2020

ALL TYPES OF ACTIVISM

O n August 28, 2020, thousands of people marched at the Lincoln Memorial in Washington, DC. Activists and other community members came together to honor the fifty-seventh anniversary of the 1963 March on Washington and to protest racial injustice.

Protests and marches are a type of activism. But Black activists can be found everywhere. They might organize community members or lead protests. Or they might research key topics or work to change laws. No matter where you find Black activists, they focus on changing systems and advocating for equal rights for all.

This book highlights the work of a small number of Black activists. Many others have led change in our nation. While some are featured in history books, most are unsung heroes.

Unsung heroes are regular people who work hard to make the world a better place.

Members of the Student Nonviolent Coordinating Committee at a 1961 meeting in Atlanta, Georgia

CHAPTER 1

EDUCATION

Education inspires the Black community to lead change. During the civil rights movement in the 1950s and 1960s, activists from the Student Nonviolent Coordinating Committee provided education through Freedom Schools. They provided basic education along with civics training. Activists continue to teach everyday people how to lift their voices for justice through education and civic engagement.

SUMMER LEARNING

Marian Wright Edelman has worked tirelessly for underserved communities since the start of her career. She started the Children's Defense Fund (CDF) in 1973. The organization created summer and after-school CDF Freedom Schools program. There are more than 150 program sites nationwide. Students develop their reading, communication, and leadership skills and more. They are inspired to lead change in their communities. In 2021 Edelman's program was serving over seven thousand students.

Marian Wright Edelman's work impacts students nationwide.

REFLECT

HEALTH AND NUTRITION

The Black Panthers knew a healthy start to each day begins with a nutritious breakfast. Black Panther Aaron Lloyd Dixon helped create the Free Breakfast for School Children Program. Dixon was one of the founders of the Seattle chapter of the Black Panthers. He dedicated a lot of time to helping local youth. Through the program, breakfasts were served in community spaces to meet the needs of local children. The Panthers made and served the meals. Students were able to listen and participate better in school after a hearty breakfast.

The Panthers started breakfast programs, such as this one in Kansas City, Missouri, across the US.

DIVERSITY IN BOOKS

Eleven-year-old Marley Dias wanted to read more books with Black girls as main characters, but she couldn't find more of them on her own. This inspired her to create the #1000BlackGirlBooks drive in 2015. She used social media to ask for recommendations and one thousand book donations from other people. She beat her goal and had collected

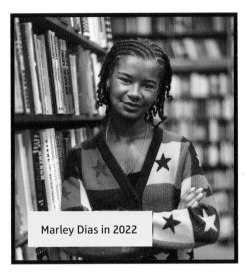

Marley Dias in 2022

thirteen thousand books by 2022. She has spoken at many events, including the White House's United State of Women with First Lady Michelle Obama and celebrity Oprah Winfrey, about what motivated her to begin her book drive.

DID YOU KNOW?

One of the first books that civil rights leader Dr. Martin Luther King Jr. appeared in was a comic book, *Martin Luther King and the Montgomery Story*. The book taught young people about nonviolent resistance strategies and provided tools to organize themselves and their communities.

CHAPTER 2
HEALTH

 lack activists recognize that equal access to health care helps keep a community strong. They work for health and wellness for everyone.

SPECIAL DELIVERY

Dr. Leonidas H. Berry fought for equal access to health care for Black communities. In the 1960s, he worked with a team to create the Flying Black Medics. The group of medical professionals flew from Chicago, Illinois, to a lower-income community in Cairo, Illinois. They delivered medicine and offered treatment. They also built a medical clinic.

Dr. Leonidas H. Berry

DID YOU KNOW?

Dr. Robert Smith helped create the nation's first rural community health center. It was built in Mound Bayou, Mississippi, in 1967. Other rural communities followed in his footsteps and created access to health care for thousands of people in need.

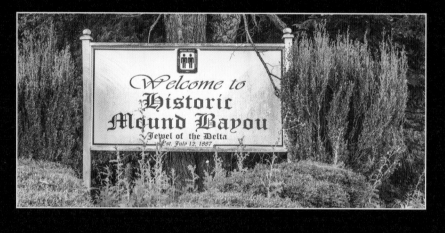

COMMUNITY HEALTH CLINICS

Fred Hampton was twenty when he joined the Chicago chapter of the Black Panthers. He was from Chicago and fought for equal rights and freedom for its communities. When the health-care needs of the Black community were not being met, Hampton took action. He created a clinic in Chicago that offered free medical care to people in need. He also helped start a free breakfast program for local students.

Fred Hampton speaks to a Chicago, Illinois, crowd in 1969.

"First you have free breakfasts, then you have free medical care, then you have free bus rides, and soon you have FREEDOM!"

—FRED HAMPTON, ACTIVIST LEADER

RACISM AND HEALTH

Racism can lead to sickness and disease due to issues such as stress or living in polluted neighborhoods. Dr. Camara Phyllis Jones seeks to identify, measure, and address the impact of racism on people's health. She has been organizing a national campaign against racism since 2015. Her educational tools help children and adults identify racism when it occurs. They also help people challenge racism and promote justice.

Neighborhoods near power plants face pollution, which can lead to health issues.

CHAPTER 3
WEALTH

Throughout US history, laws and policies have made it harder for Black people to find jobs and build wealth. Some laws have limited where Black families could live, keeping them in lower-income communities. Many Black families still face barriers when trying to find good housing, send their children to college, and meet their basic needs. Activists lead change by creating jobs and showing Black community members how to build wealth.

John Hope Bryant in 2022

BUILDING WEALTH

John Hope Bryant saw firsthand the financial challenges the Black community experiences. After the 1992 Los Angeles riots, businesses struggled to rebuild and families needed support. Bryant founded Operation Hope to help build wealth for children and families through financial education and coaching. He also helps people start businesses that create more jobs and provide services needed in their communities.

TEACHING INVESTING

Mellody Hobson grew up without a lot of money. She wanted to change her life and help others get the resources that they need to change their lives too. In college she started working at Ariel Investments. The investment firm helps people make money by investing in funds such as stocks. Hobson later became president of the firm.

Mellody Hobson speaks at the 2020 Embrace Ambition Summit. The program works to challenge stereotypes.

Hobson is a multimillionaire. She is the chair of the board of Starbucks and a part owner of the Denver Broncos football team. Her work has shown others how to grow their money as she did.

CREATING JOBS AND HELPING THE ENVIRONMENT

Mikaila Ulmer was just four years old when she founded Bee Sweet Lemonade, now called Me and the Bees Lemonade. She appeared on *Shark Tank* and received $60,000 for her company. Her lemonade is sold in bottles at grocery stores nationwide. The secret to her recipe is honey, which she uses in addition to sugar. She supports the environment by donating part of her profits to groups that work to save honeybees.

Ulmer spoke at the United State of Women Summit in 2016 and introduced President Barack Obama. She inspires other young people to start their own businesses.

Mikaila Ulmer at the United State of Women in 2016

CHAPTER 4
CRIMINAL JUSTICE

There are more Black people than white people in prison because of unfair laws and practices. Prisoners often have to work in places such as factories but are paid little money. From protecting the legal rights of people of lower incomes to ensuring fair sentencing, Black activists address issues in the criminal justice system.

UNITED PURPOSE

UNITED VOICE

UNITED POWER

JL.USA

tleadershipusa.org

nalfby2030

John Legend uses his platform to work toward criminal justice reform.

DID YOU KNOW?

Bryan Stevenson created the Equal Justice Initiative to provide legal support to people of lower incomes and underserved people. He wrote the book *Just Mercy* about the challenges facing one of his clients, and it later became a hit movie. He also created a museum and memorial site about racial justice in Montgomery, Alabama.

IMPACTED FAMILIES

Singer John Legend was impacted by the prison system. His mother was imprisoned several times when he was a child. He created the FreeAmerica program to spark a national conversation about criminal justice reform, or change. In the interactive storytelling project, people from all walks of life share how they are impacted by the prison system and how they're working to change it.

REFLECT

How do activists play a role in making change?

FAIR SENTENCING

Judge Pamela Alexander addressed the issues in sentencing that impact the Black community in a 1990 landmark Minnesota Supreme Court case, *State v. Russell*. She pointed out how one person's race can lead them to receive a harsher sentence than a defendant of another race. Change didn't happen immediately, but she made a long-lasting impact. Many years later, nationwide guidelines were changed to make sentencing fairer no matter the color of someone's skin.

JUVENILE JUSTICE

When young people enter the juvenile justice system, it increases the chance of their being imprisoned as an adult. James Bell uses his legal training to help youth who have entered the juvenile justice system. He created the W. Haywood Burns Institute, which works to make the system fairer for young people, especially Black people and other people of color. The institute has worked in twenty-three states. Through it, Bell brings together other workers such as youth advocates and judges to help youth find support in their communities. He also helps organize resources such as counseling to help them avoid entering the system again.

Judge Pamela Alexander in 2010. She helped spark
change to sentencing guidelines.

Activists helping at a food drive. Part of environmental justice is making sure people have access to food and water.

CHAPTER 5

ENVIRONMENTAL JUSTICE

Black activists motivate others to protect the environment and their communities. They focus on creating equal access to resources such as clean drinking water and unpolluted air. Their goal is to make environmental justice possible for everyone.

Mari Copeny (*center*) protests racial injustice with other community members.

YOUNG ACTIVIST

Eight-year-old Mari Copeny's community was facing a water crisis in Flint, Michigan, in 2016. She took action by writing a letter to President Obama. The president visited Flint and saw the impact of the toxic water on Flint's residents, especially its kids. This led to national efforts to bring clean, safe water to the city.

Mari is the national youth ambassador for the Climate March. She also plans to run for president in 2044.

> "My generation will fix this mess of a government. Watch us."
>
> —MARI COPENY IN A 2018 TWEET

REFLECT

TRAINING THE NEXT GENERATION

Angelou Ezeilo inspires and trains Black and other underrepresented youth to protect public lands. She founded the Greening Youth Foundation to motivate youth to make a difference in the world. She hopes to connect young people with nature while preparing them for careers in environmental conservation. She also wrote a book that teaches diverse children how to take action for environmental justice in their communities.

WALKING FOR JUSTICE

In 1971 John Francis's life was forever changed after an oil spill in the San Francisco Bay, California. He worked on cleanup efforts, and it inspired him to change his lifestyle. He decided to walk instead of driving, flying, or taking trains or motorized boats. He is known as the Planetwalker and inspires people around the world to join his efforts through his organization, Planetwalk.

ONGOING ACTIVISM

Black activists continue to work for justice and freedom. They recognize many types of activism, from protesting to community education. But action is required to make social change, no matter which tools are used. Each day, activists commit to making the world a better place.

DID YOU KNOW?

Jerome Foster II organizes youth to take action to address climate change. At eighteen, he was appointed to the White House Environmental Justice Advisory Council, making him the youngest White House adviser ever.

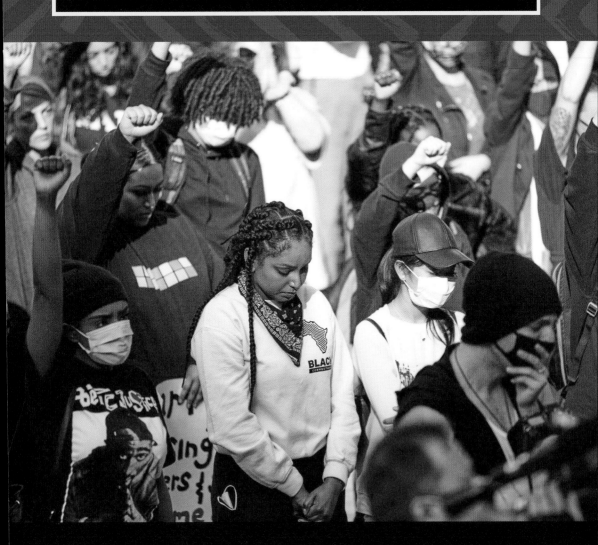

Activists such as protesters work to change the world around them.

GLOSSARY

advocate: to support or promote the interests of a cause or group

civic: of or relating to a citizen, city, or community

conservation: protecting and preserving something, such as the environment

criminal justice: the delivery of justice when a crime occurs

defendant: a person who is accused of committing a crime

environmental justice: a movement that seeks to create fair environmental policies for everyone and increase access to safer environments such as places with little pollution

juvenile justice system: the justice system impacting youth and children

nonviolent resistance: confronting injustice without the use of violence

riot: when a group challenges a system through physical force

sentence: the punishment given for a crime, often an amount of time in prison

SOURCE NOTES

13   Olivia B. Waxman, "With Free Medical Clinics and Patient Advocacy, the Black Panthers Created a Legacy in Community Health That Still Exists amid COVID-19," *Time*, February 25, 2021, https://time .com/5937647/black-panther-medical-clinics-history-school -covid-19/.

25   Mari Copeny (@LittleMissFlint), 2018, "Im 11. My generation will fix this mess of a government. Watch us." Twitter, October 6, 2018, 3:53 p.m., https://twitter.com/littlemissflint/status /1048677585704701953.

READ WOKE READING LIST

Britannica Kids: Black Panther Party
https://kids.britannica.com/kids/article/Black-Panther-Party
/632762

Britannica Kids: Marian Wright Edelman
https://kids.britannica.com/kids/article/Marian-Wright-Edelman
/623403

Cooper, Brittney. *Stand Up! Ten Mighty Women Who Made a Change*. New York: Scholastic, 2022.

Daniele, Kristina Brooke. *Civil Rights Then and Now: A Timeline of Past and Present Social Justice Issues in America*. Coral Gables, FL: Mango Media, 2022.

Dixon, Robert P., Jr. *Black Achievements in Business: Celebrating Oprah Winfrey, Moziah Bridges, and More*. Minneapolis: Lerner Publications, 2024.

Exploring the History of Freedom Schools
https://www.civilrightsteaching.org/exploring-history-freedom
-schools

National Geographic Kids: Martin Luther King Jr.
https://kids.nationalgeographic.com/history/article/martin
-luther-king-jr

Rippon, Jo. *Rise Up! The Art of Protest*. Watertown, MA: Charlesbridge, 2020.

INDEX

PHOTO ACKNOWLEDGMENTS

Image credits: Salwan Georges/The Washington Post/Getty Images, p. 4; Drazen Zigic/Shutterstock.com, p. 5; Lynn Pelham/Getty Images, p. 6; Nikki Kahn/The Washington Post/Getty Images, p. 7; AP Photo/William Straeter, p. 8; John Tlumacki/The Boston Globe/Getty Images, p. 9; monkeybusinessimages/Getty Images, p. 10; Image provided by National Library of Medicine. Scurlock Studio Records, Archives Center, National Museum of American History, Smithsonian Institution, p. 11; BHammond/Alamy Stock Photo, p. 12; Chicago Tribune file photo/Tribune News Service/Getty Images, p. 13; Liyao Xie/Getty Images, p. 14; michaeljung/Shutterstock.com, p. 15; Paras Griffin/Getty Images for Operation Hope, p. 16; Craig Barritt/Getty Images, p. 17; AP Photo/Cliff Owen, p. 18; GikaPhoto By waraphot/Shutterstock.com, p. 19; Astrid Stawiarz/Getty Images, p. 20; Andi Rice/Bloomberg/Getty Images, p. 21; ZUMA Press Inc/Alamy Stock Photo, p. 23; EnclusiveMedia/Shutterstock.com, p. 24; Jake May/MLive.com/The Flint Journal via AP, p. 25; Michal Urbanek/Shutterstock.com, p. 27.

Cover: Image provided by National Library of Medicine. Scurlock Studio Records, Archives Center, National Museum of American History, Smithsonian Institution; Derrick Salters/WENN.com/Alamy Photo.

This book is dedicated to Congressman John Lewis who taught me the importance of getting in "good trouble."

Lerner Publications Company
An imprint of Lerner Publishing Group, Inc.
241 First Avenue North
Minneapolis, MN 55401 USA

For reading levels and more information, look up this title at www.lernerbooks.com.

Main body text set in Aptifer Sans LT Pro.
Typeface provided by Linotype AG.

Editor: Lauren Foley **Designer:** Kim Morales
Lerner team: Martha Kranes

Library of Congress Cataloging-in-Publication Data

Names: Tyner, Artika R., author.
Title: Black achievements in activism : celebrating Leonidas H. Berry, Marley Dias, and more / Dr. Artika R. Tyner.
Other titles: Celebrating Leonidas H. Berry, Marley Dias, and more
Description: Minneapolis : Lerner Publications, [2024] | Series: Black Excellence Project (Read woke books) | Includes bibliographical references and index. | Audience: Ages 9–14 | Audience: Grades 4–6 | Summary: "From education to health care to the environment, Black activists work to create change and take action against injustice. Learn about Black activist leaders like Mari Copeny, Aaron Lloyd Dixon, and more"—Provided by publisher.
Identifiers: LCCN 2022033232 (print) | LCCN 2022033233 (ebook) | ISBN 9781728486611 (lib. bdg.) | ISBN 9781728496108 (eb pdf)
Subjects: LCSH: African American civil rights workers—History—Juvenile literature. | Civil rights workers—History—Juvenile literature. | African Americans—Social conditions—Juvenile literature. | Social justice—United States—Juvenile literature.
Classification: LCC E185.86 .T96 2024 (print) | LCC E185.86 (ebook) | DDC 323.089/96073—dc23/eng/20220721

LC record available at https://lccn.loc.gov/2022033232
LC ebook record available at https://lccn.loc.gov/2022033233

Manufactured in the United States of America
1-52591-50765-12/21/2022